Middle School Academic Achievement Award
presented to
HALLIE HORVATH

Head of School

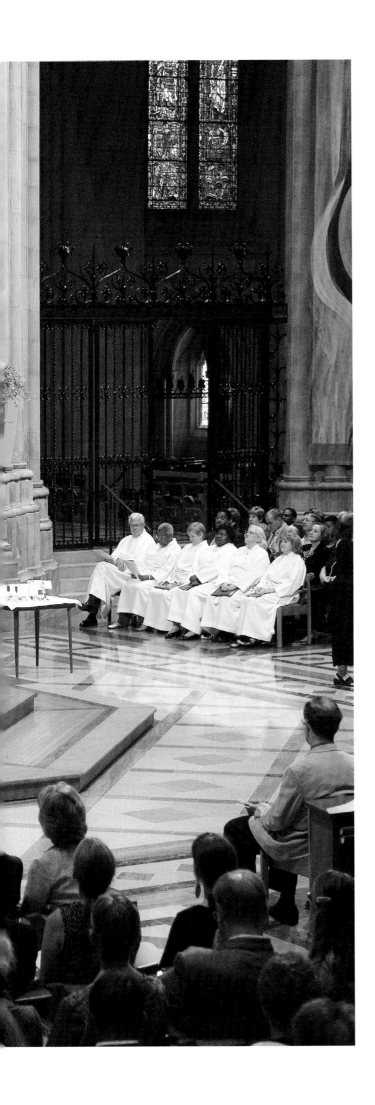

LIVING
STONES

*Washington
National
Cathedral
at 100*

Washington National Cathedral
Washington, D. C.

Living Stones: Washington National Cathedral at 100
is made possible through the generosity of
Mr. and Mrs. Joe L. Allbritton

Living Stones: Washington National Cathedral at 100
is dedicated to the
visionaries and clergy,
leaders and supporters,
artists, artisans, workers,
volunteers, and staff
whose tireless efforts
made the first 100 years possible.

Come to him, a living stone,

though rejected by mortals

yet chosen and precious in God's sight,

and like living stones,

let yourselves be built into a spiritual house,

to be a holy priesthood,

to offer spiritual sacrifices acceptable to God

through Jesus Christ.

—1 Peter 2:4–5

CONTENTS

A Cathedral for the 21st Century

One of the most telling moments in this Cathedral's life happens daily at the west front as visitors first step into the nave. If you linger near the welcome desk, you can often hear their gasps of amazement, what our docents call the "wow moment," when first-time guests are overwhelmed by what they see. They have left behind the bustle of the city and find themselves in a vast, womblike space of sweeping arches, massive piers, and cascades of multi-colored light. For nearly everyone, the Cathedral experience begins in awe—at the immensity, grandeur, and radiant beauty that surrounds them.

Some years ago Susan Howatch, a worldly author of popular novels, had just such an experience when, during a time of personal turbulence, she first saw England's Salisbury Cathedral:

> I looked out and saw this fantastic sight . . . the floodlit Cathedral, gorgeous, stunning, out of this world, certainly out of any world I'd been inhabiting. It was radiant, ravishing. I stopped dead and that was the moment when the scales fell from my eyes. I felt I had been presented with some extraordinary gift. I could now see and recognize the overpowering beauty of the Cathedral—which was the sign pointing beyond itself to the reality which was still hidden from my conscious mind . . . I was being systematically seduced by the Cathedral . . .

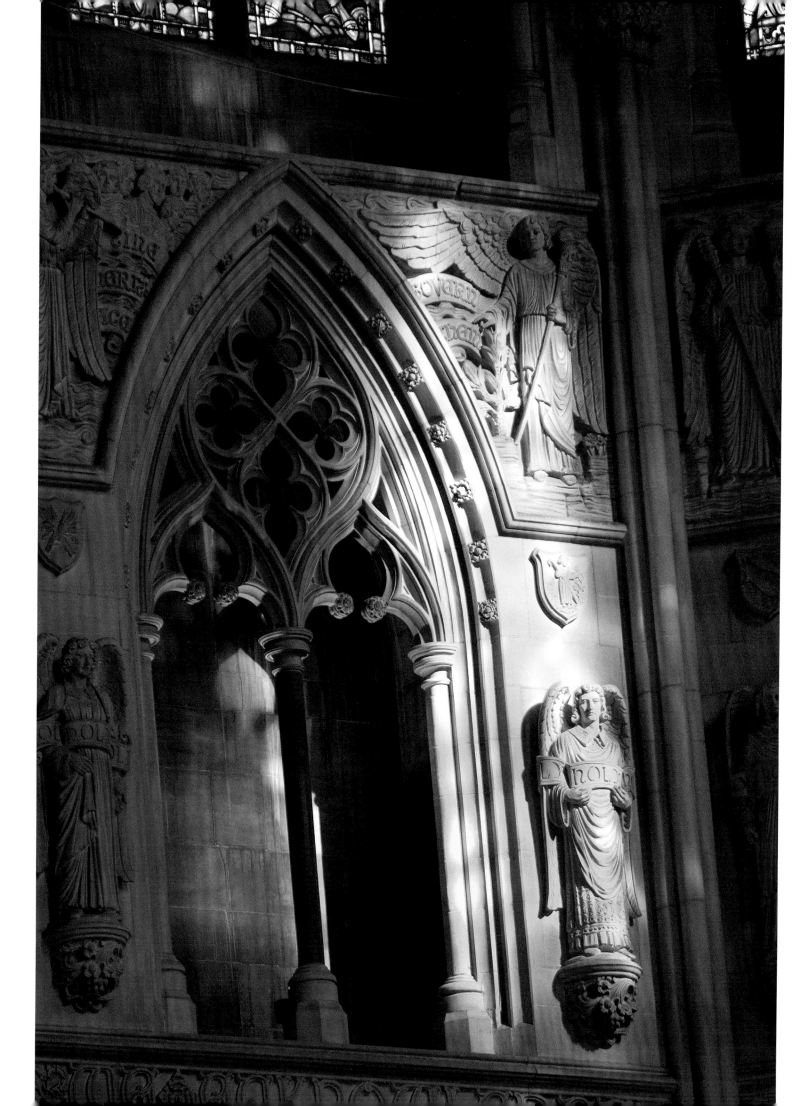

As Howatch discovered, the business of cathedrals is seduction, seeking to entice worshipers and visitors alike into a lifetime of exploring the mysterious God whose presence they sense in these sacred spaces. Into cathedrals come the curious, the seekers, the broken-hearted, and the lost. Our hope is that while they may enter this Cathedral as casual guests, they will discover they have become pilgrims, experiencing perhaps a shudder of discovery, a lump in their throat, a hunger to know more, a sense of grateful appreciation, a long-suppressed question now returning to haunt them. They may discover there was a reason to be here beyond anything they could have realized.

Cathedrals are acts of extravagance. They seek to show us a vast unity that transcends our everyday categories, inviting us to see ourselves as part of an encompassing oneness of self and cosmos. They seek to inspire in us a vision of a world held together by unity of purpose embodied in the sweeping harmony of architecture and faith. Conceived to be what one writer has called "utopian spaces," cathedrals offer a vision of heaven for people to experience in the here and now—all of life held together within the embrace of a loving God. And so in our age of fragmentation and disconnection, glimpsing such soaring grandeur and beauty can be exceedingly powerful.

Our new century will have us building "a spiritual house," a house made of the living stones of people worshiping, praying, studying, living the Christian faith, embodying Christ's love in this city and beyond.

In the Middle Ages, when most of the cathedrals of Europe were built, these magnificent structures often served secular as well as religious purposes. Many were originally conceived as destinations for pilgrims coming to pray in the presence of the relics of saints, and often began as monasteries. But these immense structures quickly took on multiple uses as public markets, courts of law, and town halls. Townspeople sometimes bustled through the cavernous buildings among clucking poultry, braying livestock, and busy merchants, while overhead angelic hosts carved in stone seemed to take flight and glimmering light poured through the stained glass. Off in the distance a choir of monks might be heard

chanting their prayers, as pilgrims arrived to light a candle and linger in a quiet side chapel.

Today, the notion of "cathedral" has expanded in unimagined ways—as pilgrims and visitors can "travel" to our Cathedral via the Internet, or on their iPods, joining us in worship and in our many programs. And so as we welcome each day hundreds of visitors and seekers arriving through our west doors, we often welcome thousands by way of our website.

Washington National Cathedral was founded by a visionary group of Episcopalians at the beginning of the 20th century. These founders, led by Bishop Henry Yates Satterlee, committed themselves to building a spiritual home for a robust young nation. It would be located at one of the highest points in the city, overlooking the halls of government, the monuments, the symbols of the nation's life. Indeed, a visitor to the nation's capital would see a city presided over by two prominent hills, on one the U.S. Capitol, where the destiny of the country is shaped, and on the other the nation's house of prayer. Building the Cathedral would require 83 years, a vast commitment of artistic vision, hard labor, financial generosity, and sense of purpose.

Bishop Satterlee and his colleagues launched Washington National Cathedral with three specific missions: to be "a house of prayer for all people," "the chief mission church of the diocese," and "a church intended for national purposes." All have remained important signposts in our life. We know that, for many, building this Cathedral was an act of Christian love, and of patriotism as well. They believed that amid all the great buildings and monuments in the nation's capital, one of them should represent the God whom they believed loved and had a mission for America. They yearned for a more united country and a more united church, and they believed this Cathedral could be a symbol and force for such unity.

This new church grew into the wide array of roles a cathedral has traditionally played as a spiritual center serving city, diocese, and in this case, nation, in a way that local churches and parishes could not. With inspired foresight, Bishop Satterlee enumerated some of our most vital missions, among them to be "a watch tower from which the signs of the time are detected" and "a home of religious learning" where theologians would translate the "truths of theology in the common language of life." The Cathedral embraced these roles and more as it became increasingly a center for the sacred arts, a forum for debate and discussion, a platform for prophetic proclamation, a place of quiet solace and meditation, and a destination for pilgrimage and spiritual transformation.

This new church grew into the wide array of roles a cathedral has traditionally played as a spiritual center serving city, diocese, and in this case, nation, in a way that local churches and parishes could not.

As the Cathedral building slowly took shape through the twentieth century, so too did its national mission as a sacred place to which the nation can turn in times of crisis and celebration. It was here that President Woodrow Wilson was buried in 1924, and through the years nearly every president has been honored with a funeral or memorial service here. In recent years the nation turned to this Cathedral as it mourned the deaths of Presidents Reagan and Ford. In the dark days following the terrorist attack of September 11, 2001, all eyes focused on the service at the National Cathedral. And so it has gone—with interfaith services of prayers for peace in the Middle East, for the victims of Hurricane Katrina, for ending global poverty.

This book has been created as part of our centennial celebration, to honor the courage and devotion of the dreamers and builders of our first

century, who created not only one of the most beautiful buildings in our country, but shaped programs and ministries that continue to inspire our work today. It is meant to celebrate the foundation, securely laid in our extraordinary building and grounds, for the vital work of our second century.

As we move into the next hundred years, we are being guided by a fresh vision of the Cathedral's mission. After a first century devoted to carving a glorious church out of Indiana limestone, now we are able to devote our energies to a new kind of construction. For this we have taken as our guide a passage from the New Testament, "Come to him, a living stone, . . . and like living stones, let yourselves be built into a spiritual house, . . . to offer spiritual sacrifices acceptable to God through Jesus Christ."

Our new century will have us building "a spiritual house," a house made of the living stones of people worshiping, praying, studying, living the Christian faith, embodying Christ's love in this city and beyond. Our challenge is to be as bold, visionary, and courageous in this new century of "spiritual" construction as our forebears were with the stone and glass of the first.

Our hope is that while they may enter this Cathedral as casual guests, they will discover they have become pilgrims, experiencing perhaps a shudder of discovery, a lump in their throat, a hunger to know more, a sense of grateful appreciation, a long-suppressed question now returning to haunt them.

The world needs these grand and ancient-seeming cathedrals more than ever. It needs these massive signs of God's presence in the world, these places of mystery and beauty, these powerful forces for unity and healing in its cities. And in this dangerous and divided 21st century, our world needs what cathedrals are perhaps uniquely in a position to offer—a vigorous voice of a generous-spirited Christian faith capable of engaging the public imagination.

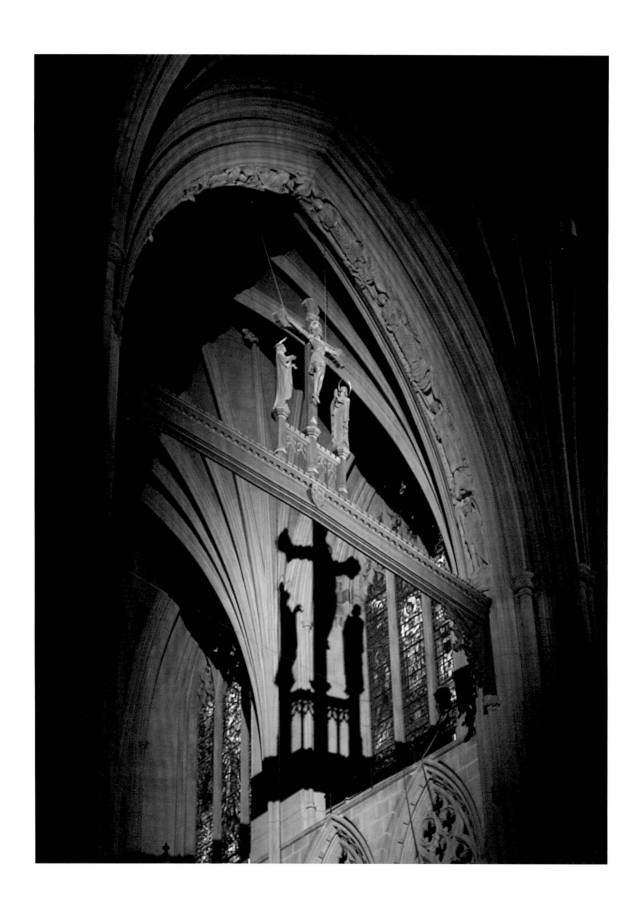

A key missing element in our world's public discourse is an open-minded, intellectually probing, compassionate Christianity. We believe this Cathedral is called to be a strong voice of a faith that is firm at the center and soft at the edges, deeply rooted in the tradition and profoundly open and welcoming, a faith that embraces ambiguity, that honors other faiths, that insists that Christian values be embodied in the social order.

Central to our life and mission is the work of reconciliation. Our world and its many religions are riddled with conflict and division. The need for a sacred place that is working to bring people of all faiths and convictions together to engage in genuine dialogue has never been more urgent. And our Cathedral must participate vigorously with our interfaith friends in the efforts of our day to ease the suffering from extreme poverty and disease across the globe.

We believe we are called, too, to sustain a courageous prophetic voice challenging the public life of our time with the vision of God's justice and compassion that we encounter in our scriptures. In our first century, memorable preachers and prophets used our Canterbury Pulpit to address the nation. Dr. Martin Luther King, Jr., preached his final Sunday sermon from that pulpit before he was assassinated in Memphis. The 14th Dalai Lama, the Rev. Billy Graham, President Jimmy Carter, and others have articulated their beliefs from that same pulpit. In the Cathedral's own life, Dean Francis Sayre and Bishop John Walker exercised powerful prophetic ministries.

The world needs these grand and ancient-seeming cathedrals more than ever. It needs these massive signs of God's presence in the world, these places of mystery and beauty, these powerful forces for unity and healing in its cities.

Day by day the routines of Cathedral life go on—in public prayer, hospitality, and service. Each day we offer multiple worship services, and each day visitors stream in to explore the riches of art and faith. In the course of our ministry, theologians teach classes, worshipers pray for healing, conferences address the problems of war and peace, and the bridges that can be built among the religions.

This magnificent structure is completed, but Washington National Cathedral will never be finished. Standing at the heart of Washington, D.C., this Cathedral enters its second century committed to being a sign of hope and healing for the nation and the world.

After a first century devoted to carving a glorious church out of Indiana limestone, now we are able to devote our energies to a new kind of construction.

This holy place will continue to explore new and creative ways to serve as a spiritual home to our nation, embracing the challenges and opportunities as the United States becomes more religiously, racially, and ethnically diverse. It will continue to offer the nation a thoughtful, gracious Christian faith, as it expands its efforts in interfaith dialogue and service. It will continue to pray for our nation, as it holds up a vision of a world of hope and peace that comes from the heart of our faith.

Foremost and always, this Cathedral will continue to welcome strangers into our midst, and invite them to become fellow pilgrims and friends.

—Samuel T. Lloyd III

"For making us your children
by adoption and grace,
and refreshing us day by day
with the bread of life.
We thank you, Lord."

—The Book of Common Prayer

Washington Cathedral   South Elevation
Philip Hubert Frohman F·A·I·A· Architect.

"Eternal God, the heaven
of heavens cannot contain you,
much less the walls of temples
made with hands. . . .
Accept the work of our hands,
offered to your honor and glory."

—The Book of Common Prayer

To Excel All Others

HOW THE CATHEDRAL CAME TO BE GOTHIC

Cadences of a revival brought the crowd to its feet on a chilly night in 2006. A visiting preacher from Brooklyn, the Rev. Dr. Johnny Ray Youngblood, spoke about a verse so familiar that its implications might go unnoticed: "Thou preparest a table before me in the presence of mine enemies" (Psalm 23:5).

"A table!" the preacher cried out. "He doesn't dig moats, he doesn't build fences with barbed wire, he doesn't put sentries there with bayonets. God's love is for us and our enemies! He prepares tables…" Youngblood's words rang forth among the piers and intricate vaulting of the nave, rousing worshipers from the whole Eastern seaboard to help rebuild New Orleans after Hurricane Katrina.

This revival was one of innumerable worship services, performances, festivals, conferences, and tours that took place in the Cathedral's first century. As varied as these occasions are, one thing binds them: the setting. The Cathedral is unmistakably a house of prayer for all people.

The site and architecture of the Cathedral were chosen with utmost care to mark it as a holy place for all of God's children. Henry Yates Satterlee, first bishop of the Episcopal Diocese of Washington, wrote in urging construction of a cathedral, that

> . . . a house of prayer for all people means not only a House of
> God where all people are welcome, but where all people can
> join in a service, in which while they pray with the spirit, they
> pray with . . . understanding also; not only a church where all
> the congregation sing praises with understanding, but a church
> which unites every congregation in every place, with the people
> of God in all ages.

The only possible architectural style for such a project, according to Satterlee, was Gothic. A Gothic cathedral amidst buildings of religious and educational purpose—a city on a hill, in the Gospel imagery—would become his life's vision.

Before Satterlee arrived in Washington, however, quite a lot of planning had already taken place. All of it in a very different direction.

Earliest consideration of a cathedral in Washington did not touch on its architectural style. Instead, discussion centered on whether or not the capital should even have a cathedral.

For decades after the United States won independence, Episcopalians viewed the notion of a cathedral askance. It called to mind the yoke of British rule and high-church worship. Some Anglicans in the young United States had broken with the Church of England and formed the Episcopal Church amid controversy. The denomination retained many Anglican traditions; but, as patriotic Americans, Episcopalians shied away from the trappings of the Church of England. Until the 1880s, only two Episcopal houses of worship had been conceived and built as cathedrals, that is, as the seats of bishops in their dioceses. Another handful of churches had later been designated as cathedrals.

Toward the end of the 19th century, however, Americans in general grew more certain of their role in the world. Episcopalians no longer thought an American cathedral would be a pallid imitation of Old World structures. Potential was seen to adapt and improve upon a European means of glorifying God. Boston architect Ralph Adams Cram wrote in praise of cathedrals:

> Here are gathered together in organic unity all the arts of man.
> Architecture forms the setting and the shrine . . . paintings
> and statues and stained glass, tapestries, carved and gilded

woodwork, wrought metals, gold, silver, bronze, iron complete the primal architectural idea . . . And this vast and inspired creation is in no sense "art for art's sake," it is art (the ideal of beauty realized) for the sake of God's people and as the testimony of weak and fallible man to His glory.

Many Episcopalians of the day shared a similar affection for grand church buildings. They believed that American churches could express the nation's growing influence, and even hold up the United States as a moral beacon to the rest of the world.

This desire was especially felt in the nation's capital. Washington's Episcopal leaders believed that a juncture of civic and religious power might lead the country to an awakening of Christian fervor. What better start than a magnificent cathedral in the heart of the city? Moreover, they simply needed the room. Local Episcopal churches were crowded on Sundays and becoming more so each year.

The site and architecture of the Cathedral were chosen with utmost care to mark it as a holy place for all of God's children.

Two local rectors took action. In October 1890, the Rev. George Douglas of St. John's Church Lafayette Square, and the Rev. Randolph McKim of the Church of the Epiphany, addressed the question of establishing a Cathedral Foundation to Bishop William Paret of Maryland. At that time, Washington, D.C., was part of the Diocese of Maryland; it remained so until the creation of the Diocese of Washington in 1895. Douglas and McKim gathered others to their cause, including banker Charles Glover, newspaper publisher Theodore Noyes, and real estate developer George Truesdell, a member of the city's governing board.

Paret eventually approved the plan. In January 1893, the U.S. Congress issued a charter incorporating the Protestant Episcopal Cathedral Foundation. It should be noted that many foundations and companies during that era were incorporated in this manner. Congressional charters denote no relationship with the federal government.

Everything was in place to begin the project.

Now came the heart of the matter: choosing the site, the architect, and the architectural style.

The site had to be within the city proper, for easy access and prominence among major buildings. The Cathedral had to be in a part of the

city that would remain influential and not be passed by as the city moved in another direction, as cities are wont to do. Ten acres or more were required. The trustees envisioned the Cathedral as a national moral center point, which would need land for schools, a library, and housing and meeting facilities for clergy.

The Cathedral's founders drew much inspiration from Pierre L'Enfant's original 1791 plan for the city of Washington, which called for

> . . . a church intended for national purposes, such as public prayer, thanksgivings, funeral orations &c and assigned to the special use of no particular Sect or denomination, but equally open to all.

The Cathedral reflects some of L'Enfant's intentions. Although built as an Episcopal house of worship, the Cathedral fulfills the public purposes and reflects the openness that he espoused. The site L'Enfant proposed, however, was occupied by the 1890s. The U.S. Patent Office had already been built at Eighth and F Streets, N.W.; it was later occupied by the Smithsonian American Art Museum.

Land at Dupont Circle was briefly considered, but deemed too small for the anticipated crowds. Other properties were examined, and eventually fourteen acres on upper Connecticut Avenue, N.W.—then a dirt road— were chosen. Several prospective donors promptly withdrew their pledges, skeptical that worshipers would travel so far from the city's center, at least not until a trolley line had been constructed.

Time passed. The Episcopal Diocese of Washington was created. The Foundation began to incur debts, and the Connecticut Avenue commitment looked shaky.

In 1895, before Satterlee was consecrated as bishop, the trustees commissioned Ernest Flagg, who was designing Washington's Corcoran Gallery of Art, to draw up plans for a cathedral. Flagg had trained at France's École des Beaux-Arts, which emphasized structural rationality, or the ordered relationship of a building's spatial elements.

Flagg submitted two cathedral designs—one Gothic, the other Renaissance—and expressed a preference for the latter. Flagg believed that Gothic architecture was not in tune with the needs of modern churches. A long nave and large piers, characteristic of Gothic design, might obstruct views and acoustics. Not so with the wide open space and dome of his proposed Renaissance structure.

Most of the trustees thought that Flagg's Renaissance design, formally accepted in January 1896, would achieve their stated aims. The trustees envisioned the Cathedral as a prayer in stone, an acknowledgement of the majesty and benevolence of the one, true God. They anticipated the

building's practical role as a spiritual home for the nation, a center of religious thought and moral guidance. Flagg's work was featured on the cover of *Harper's Weekly,* and it was assumed that the new bishop would proceed with the plan.

This was where matters stood when Satterlee was consecrated bishop in March 1896.

Satterlee found the Connecticut Avenue land unsuitable and chose instead a site even farther from the city center. Mount St. Alban, one of Washington's highest hills, overlooks the city's monuments and neighborhoods. Satterlee understood the innate power of a cathedral rising above the city, visible to the people below as its towers reached toward heaven.

The site on Mount St. Alban, purchased in 1898 for $245,000, comprised 27 acres. Thirty acres were later added, for a total price of $291,427.

With Flagg's Renaissance design still under consideration, Satterlee began working toward his goal of building a Gothic cathedral. He described principles that guide the Cathedral's ministry today:

> It is ours, in this time and generation . . . to make real in our
> thought and action the grandeur of our ideal, in its many-sided

possibilities and opportunities; in its organisation and its work; in its spiritual influence and practical usefulness.

Why choose Gothic? Again, quoting Satterlee:

> [A] genuine Gothic Cathedral on this side of the Atlantic . . . will kindle the same religious, devotional feelings and historic associations which are awakened in the breasts of American travellers by the great Gothic cathedrals of Europe . . . American Churchmen are so weary of designs which glorify the originality of the architect, that they are longing more and more for a pure Gothic Church which is built simply for the Glory of God.

Satterlee knew much about the Gothic Revival, which had been in full swing for decades. The movement began with England's Church Building Act of 1818. Although neo-Classical architecture was more popular at that time, Gothic churches were found to be less expensive to build.

"The Cathedral would be much more than simply a church; it would be part of the fabric of America's moral leadership."

Gothic design also benefited from the Romantic movement, which looked back longingly to simpler times. The Industrial Revolution, accompanied by social upheavals, was exhilarating but frightening. People felt that machines were dehumanizing society. Change was happening too quickly. The Middle Ages signified perfect order, an era uncontaminated with the chaos of new ideas, untainted by the secularism of the Renaissance.

Gothic style was further promoted by the critic John Ruskin and the Pre-Raphaelites, such as William Morris and Edward Burne-Jones, who decorated the churches designed by the renowned English Gothicist George F. Bodley. In America, proponents included Ralph Cram and Henry Vaughan, who had worked as George Bodley's chief draftsman.

By the time these devotees finished their work, it was said that more (neo-)Gothic structures were built during the Revival period than during the original Gothic period of the 12th through 14th centuries.

Enthusiasm for the delicately ornate Gothic style was fostered by artists who opposed industrialization. They hoped the past could somehow be prologue, fed by new wisdom and an advanced artistic sensibility. Among these artists was Charles E. Kempe, whose stained glass windows now grace Bethlehem Chapel at Washington National Cathedral.

Another influence on Gothic Revival style was the Decorative Arts movement, later the Arts and Crafts movement, which promoted an abundance of decorative elements inside and outside churches. This influence is reflected in the Cathedral's iron, textiles, wood, and sculpture.

Finally, the Gothic Revival period emphasized landscaping that broke away from the ordered style of rows of trees and symmetrically placed promenades. Landscape designers now emulated the unpredictable order of nature. The winding paths, lakes, and clusters of trees in Central Park, designed by Frederick Law Olmsted, Sr., offer a fine example. Olmsted's sons brought this same sensibility to the grounds of the Cathedral: Olmsted Woods is a natural preserve from which visitors emerge to behold the "prayer in stone" rising above.

Ultimately the Cathedral and its grounds (known as the Close) together evoked the rebirth of Gothic style and the artistic and societal movements that attended it. To what extent did prevailing tastes and movements affect Bishop Satterlee's preference for Gothic? His writings give little insight. Satterlee was an educated, well-read, and well-traveled man, who had seen the great cathedrals of Europe. He probably knew of the many-layered aesthetics behind the Gothic Revival and the ways in which Gothic symbolism related to what he and the Cathedral's founders were trying to achieve.

The trustees were also educated, well-read, and well-traveled. They knew of the building boom in America's great cities. The first skyscrapers were being built in New York and Chicago. The Brooklyn Bridge, that marvel of engineering and artistry with Gothic arches rising 300 feet above the river, had opened in 1883.

Simply by strolling around Washington, these gentlemen could see all the popular architectural styles of the day. The Classical design of the White House contrasted with its flamboyant Beaux-Arts neighbor, now called the Eisenhower Executive Office Building. The Gothic-style Smithsonian castle had been completed in 1855, the Washington Monument obelisk in 1884, and the Italian Renaissance–style Library of Congress in 1897. New mansions around Dupont Circle were a mixture of Beaux-Arts, Romanesque, and Classical.

Movements were afoot to bring order as well as beauty to the city. In 1901, the McMillan Commission (including Daniel Burnham, the "dean" of American architecture; Charles F. McKim, of one of New York's leading architectural firms; and Frederick Law Olmsted, Jr.) presented a report to Congress on beautifying the nation's capital, starting with the creation of the Mall.

Flagg's design for a Renaissance-style cathedral, although accepted by the trustees two months before Satterlee's consecration, had never captured much enthusiasm. It was abandoned.

During the next decade, Satterlee quietly campaigned for a Gothic structure, while the trustees joined him in the hard work of raising funds to build it. Now the decision was made to appoint an advisory committee to help the bishop and trustees make three important decisions: where on the grounds to place the building, whether there should be an architectural competition, and what architectural style should be adopted.

The committee made two firm recommendations: that the building be placed on the northeast side of Mount St. Alban, and that there be no architectural competition. The question of style hung stubbornly in the air.

It now seems curious, given Satterlee's indefatigable support of Gothic architecture, that a few proponents of Classic Renaissance had been named to the committee. This august minority went down to defeat, but not quietly. In a thank-you letter to Daniel Burnham, Satterlee wrote that the trustees had decided to follow the committee's two firm recommendations,

> but, regarding the architectural style, as this subject had been before the Cathedral Chapter and under very careful consideration for ten years, the former decision was affirmed, that the style should be Gothic.

Or, as Satterlee stated elsewhere, "Gothic is God's style."
On May 21, 1906, the trustees passed a resolution stating that

> . . . while fully recognizing the beauties of classic style, [it] sees no reason why it should change its views as originally enunciated, and therefore adheres to its decision that the Gothic style shall be adopted.

When completed, Washington National Cathedral would be described as principally in the style of English Decorated Gothic, with aspects of French (the West Front) and Spanish (the South Transept portal) Gothic.

Once the architectural style was formally selected, events began to move more quickly. The final decision was the choice of an architect. Satterlee felt strongly that success depended upon the architect's

> . . . religious enthusiasm, his architectural knowledge, the creative ability he has displayed, his experience in construction, his adaptability, executive power and similar characteristics.

Satterlee traveled to England to find the finest Gothic architect of the day, and was repeatedly advised to seek out George Frederick Bodley.

In 1906, Bodley was perhaps the leading Gothicist among English architects. He was also a published poet, a composer, and organist. A business he established with two other architects to design wallpaper and textiles, Watts & Co., continues to this day. Bodley was a jovial extrovert, a husband and father, and a devout Anglican.

When Bishop Satterlee reached him, Bodley was working as the superintendent architect for Liverpool Cathedral and the supervising architect for York Minster. He was 79 years old. As Satterlee prepared to return to America, Bodley wrote to him, in July 1906:

> The opportunity that your coming Cathedral will afford is vast for good. It would be grand if your newer world in America should show the world that the ancient dignity and beauty of religious Christian architecture can be achieved in these days. It could be so. Gothic art with all its acceptance of the beauty of nature, as its basis, and its added spiritual, aspiring, fervour could do all this.

Bodley touched on a point of much concern to Satterlee, that the Cathedral not merely imitate, but that it continue an evolving architectural style that would live on and reflect the most highly developed Christian sensibilities of any age in which it appeared.

In September, the bishop wrote Bodley, asking if he would be amenable "to act with an American Architect." Bodley agreed to be the leading architect, "meaning thereby that the initiative of the design should be chiefly my work."

Satterlee wanted an American partner for Bodley because only an American could understand American tastes and culture, and because donors would more willingly support a cathedral with an American pedigree.

The bishop chose Henry Vaughan. Although English-born, Vaughan had lived in the United States for 25 years. According to his biographer William Morgan, Vaughan came to America determined to bring pure English Gothic to the Episcopal Church. A devout Anglo-Catholic, Vaughan believed that architecture and religion were two sides of the same coin. Vaughan was shy, a bachelor. His work was his life. In 1906, he was 61 years old.

Bodley and Vaughan were commissioned to create a plan for Satterlee to present to the trustees. Although the architects worked in partnership, correspondence makes clear that Bodley was the principal designer.

Satterlee actively joined discussions about what the design would and would not include. The bishop chose the name of the great central tower,

Gloria In Excelsis, evoking the Incarnation, God made man, a basic tenet of Christian faith and of the intended iconography. Bodley suggested a Nativity Chapel, which became Bethlehem Chapel.

"Eternity lies at the heart of a cathedral."

The two men actively corresponded about specific details and broad philosophical points. The architect objected to "excess of richness," preferring "much dignity and a solemn grandeur . . . so do not expect too ornate a building." Satterlee responded that he agreed, up to a point, but added,

> . . . we must remember on the other hand that in raising funds for the Cathedral everything will depend upon the way in which the designs meet with general approval and inspire enthusiasm. . . . You yourself will know just how far richness of ornamentation will create this feeling of gladness in the beholder. . . . I earnestly trust that in the effort for solemnity and grandeur there will not be the appearance of austerity or heaviness.

The choice of stone for construction brought about much debate. Bodley and Vaughan wanted a red stone, Satterlee a cream-colored stone. The bishop's choice prevailed. The building committee settled on Indiana oolitic limestone.

On June 8, 1907, Vaughan presented the plans to the trustees. Two days later, they voted to accept the Bodley-Vaughan design.

The proposed structure was 476 feet long and 132 feet wide, with transepts, a choir terminating in a five-sided apse, two chapels, a nave consisting of five aisles and nine bays, a narthex and twin towers on the west façade, an octagonal baptistry off the southwest end of the nave, and dominating it all the Gloria In Excelsis tower, rising 258 feet.

As pleased as Satterlee was with the overall design, he voiced trepidation about the West Front, which he felt was "too gloomy and austere"; it "repels rather than invites." He urged Bodley to make it "less heavy" by including "a good deal more of a broken surface, more light and shadow, more of traceried effect between the top of the central arch and the peak of the Nave roof." The façade was set almost at ground level. Returning to his vision of "a city set on a hill," Satterlee recommended that steps be added.

Although Satterlee's criticisms disappointed Bodley, he wrote that he was "enriching the façade" in revisions of the plan.

On September 29, 1907, the foundation stone was laid. Canon Richard Feller, clerk of the works for more than forty years, includes this description in his book *For Thy Great Glory:*

> On hand was the mallet George Washington used in the laying of the cornerstone of the United States Capitol . . . Bishop Satterlee placed the mortar, and made in it the sign of the cross with the point of his trowel. The Stone lies directly beneath the High Altar. Striking the Stone three times with the Washington mallet, he made the declaration of dedication, then all the choirs and people joined in and sang *Gloria in Excelsis.*

Standing beside the bishop was Henry Vaughan. A few weeks after this ceremony, on October 12, George Bodley died. In December, Henry Vaughan was officially designated sole architect of the Cathedral.

Vaughan continued to alter plans for the west front and address Satterlee's concerns that the building would be too small. Ultimately, Vaughan's work on Bethlehem Chapel was his most appreciated contribution. He modified Bodley's design, deleting the ambulatory behind the apse because he did not want anything to block light to the chapel. This alteration yielded an unusual feature: completely free-standing buttresses surrounding the apse.

Henry Yates Satterlee died on February 22, 1908. He had literally worn himself out in his efforts to build the Cathedral. Although others designed the structure, Satterlee's stamp is on every architectural detail because of his close work with Bodley on the original design, and because his sheer force of will created this "prayer in stone."

When Henry Vaughan died in June 1917, the trustees again faced the huge task of finding an architect. After several years of considering major architects nationwide, in 1921 the trustees designated the firm of Frohman, Robb and Little.

Although accomplished in their field, these were young men: Philip Frohman was 34, Harry B. Little, 39, and E. Donald Robb, 41. To offset any concerns about the extent of the firm's experience, the trustees named Ralph Adams Cram as consulting architect. Cram was also designing the nave of the Cathedral Church of St. John the Divine in New York. Limitations on his time, and growing disputes with Frohman over changes to the Bodley-Vaughan design, led to a parting of the ways. After Robb and Little died in the 1940s, Frohman became the sole architect.

Today, Philip Frohman is most clearly identified with the Cathedral's architecture. The work of Bodley and Vaughan provided a sure foundation. Frohman, in consultation with Deans George C. F. Bratenahl and Francis Sayre, Jr., and with the trustees' approval, created the final design.

Frohman lengthened the nave by forty feet and increased the height of the Gloria In Excelsis tower by 42 feet. He added chapels, galleries and aisles in both transepts, a north porch, and the cloister-garth. Row asserts that Frohman's changes most dramatically affected the west front. Alterations included a large rose window instead of a recessed wheel window, the addition of niches, balconies, and canopies, an increase in the height of the west towers by 34 feet, the broadening of the façade to be substantially wider than the nave, and the elimination of an open porch.

When Philip Frohman died in October 1972, the nave was not complete; it would be dedicated in 1976. The West End had yet to be started. But those who devote their lives to building a cathedral do not expect to see its completion. When the last finial was set on September 29, 1990, those in attendance had a sense of connecting with the many whose labors, generosity, and vision had created an exquisite sacred space.

Eternity lies at the heart of a cathedral. This is the gift of Gothic architecture: a sense of *kairos*, of non-linear time that allows reaching across the centuries to bring all into communion in prayerful awe of the forgiving and eternal love of God for his creatures. This is God's gift.

—*Diane Ney*

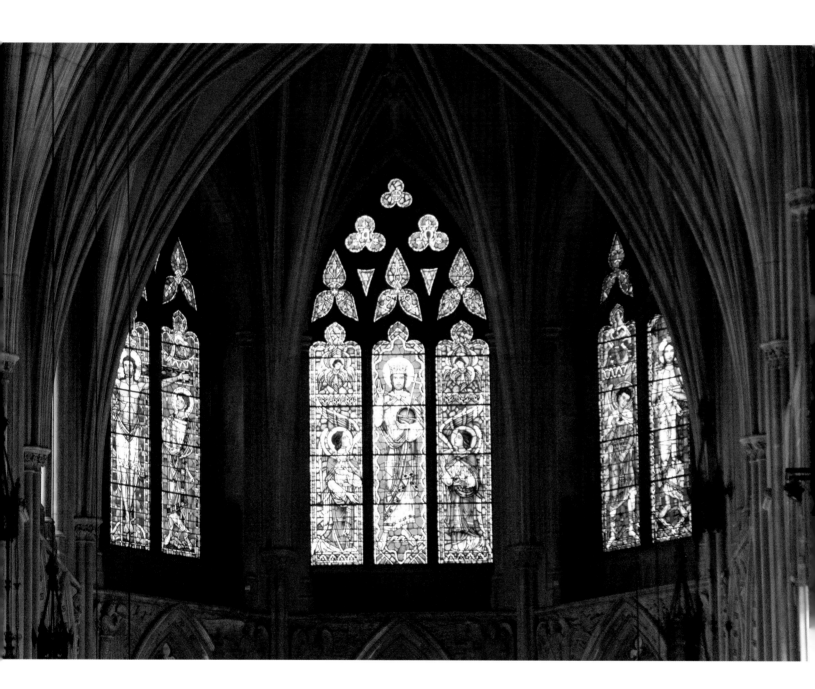

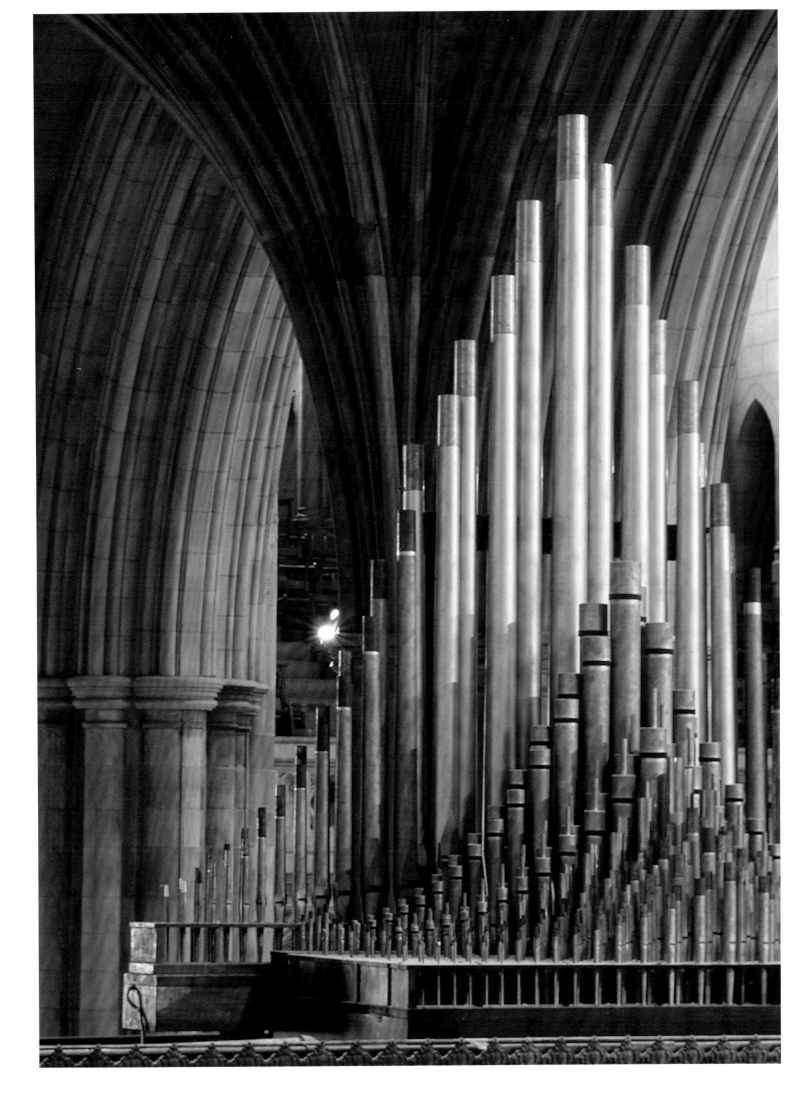

HIDDEN ETERNITY
MARKING A SACRED SPACE

The people came up out of the Jordan on the tenth day of the
first month, and they camped in Gilgal on the east border of
Jericho. Those twelve stones, which they had taken out of the
Jordan, Joshua set up in Gilgal, saying to the Israelites, "When
your children ask their parents in time to come, 'What do these
stones mean?' then you shall let your children know."

Joshua 4:19–22a

Tens of thousands witnessed the laying of the Cathedral's foundation
stone a century ago. What did they see? What did they envision? The
stone itself, deliberately hidden from view in 1907, reveals much about the
Cathedral's first builders. It also holds considerable mystery.

The foundation stone differs from all others at the Cathedral, most ob-
viously in its composition. It consists of two stones, one embedded within
another. The smaller stone, possibly about one cubic foot in size, was
quarried in the Middle East, in a field adjoining the Church of the Holy
Nativity in Bethlehem, where tradition holds that Jesus of Nazareth was
born. Inscribed on one face of this stone is a passage from the Gospel of
John: "The Word was made flesh, and dwelt among us" (1:14). This stone
was set flush into a pocket carved in the surface of the second stone, a slab
of American granite about four feet by six feet by two feet.

> "Holiness can be seen to spread
> from the foundation stone to the
> whole Cathedral, much as a small
> bit of yeast spreads out among other
> ingredients in the making of bread."

This composite stone was meant to provide a practical, yet noticeably
different, purpose from most typical building stones. Instead of serving
as a cornerstone (the first stone that is traditionally laid in a building), this

foundation stone would bear great structural responsibility. Soon it carried the enormous weight of the stone altar and reredos directly above it, in Bethlehem Chapel in the crypt. Later it bore the load of the magnificent stone Jerusalem Altar two stories above, in the apse of the Cathedral's nave.

After the dedication service, the foundation stone was completely encased in surrounding foundations, with the specific intention that it would never again be dislodged or exposed to view.

All of this begs the question, why? Why create an elaborate, massive stone, whose sole purpose is to support an object used in worship (rather than an exterior wall), and then celebrate its installation with great pomp and ceremony, only to bury it, so that no one will ever see it again?

The provenance of the smaller stone, Bethlehem, reveals part of the answer. Consider an outlook that accepts the notion that inanimate objects can be vehicles of spiritual energy. An argument can be made for an inherent human need to create and invest concrete objects with important intangible principles or beliefs that go beyond superstition and sentimentality. In religious traditions, such a pattern of belief is known as "sanctification"; common material objects are set apart and made special because they are believed to have been infused with a divine spirit. Something ordinary is transformed into something extraordinary.

The stone from Bethlehem, a natural product of the earth's crust, existed at the same place and time as Jesus. A Christian might reason that it witnessed his presence. Perhaps Jesus even touched this stone. Many Christians would believe that this stone's proximity to Jesus endowed it with significance, a degree of sacredness. It is no longer common but holy. This object will retain its holiness unless deliberate action deconsecrates it or sees its divine spirit removed.

This stone from the Holy Land was set into a massive block of indigenous American rock, with the practical intent to protect the smaller stone from damage by the tremendous loads it was about to bear, but also for its ability to carry symbolic weight.

Holiness can be seen to spread from the foundation stone to the whole Cathedral, much as a small bit of yeast spreads out among other ingredients in the making of bread. The yeast both permeates and supports the dough so that loaves can be formed, baked, and consumed. Incorporating sacred objects, such as the stone from Bethlehem, into a building is meant to infuse divine energy into a new structure. Such a practice

"O God, who wonderfully created, and yet more wonderfully restored, the dignity of human nature: Grant that we may share the divine life of him who humbled himself to share our humanity, your Son, Jesus Christ . . ."

—The Book of Common Prayer

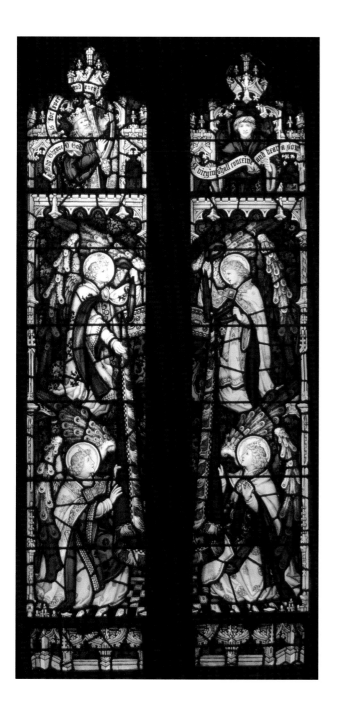

emerges from a viewpoint that understands creation, in its fundamental state, as being *profane*—not impure, but mundane, lacking the divine presence. The contrasting state is *sacred*: the divine presence is made known to humankind. Mircea Eliade, in his landmark book, *The Sacred and the Profane*, described the sacred as "always manifest[ing] itself as a reality of a wholly different order from 'natural' realities." Sacred things become points of reference, providing value, structure, and certainty in an otherwise chaotic existence.

Believers might try to promote, or facilitate, the transformation of the profane into the sacred. If this transformation is to happen, the profane must be infused with the divine spirit. Humans are incapable of containing and controlling the movements of the divine. Likewise, significant amounts of time are needed for a place or object to be invested with and recognized for its deep sanctity. Practices were therefore devised to encourage the process. One method was to take stones from places recognized as sacred, saturated with the divine spirit, and transplant or graft them onto a new place. These stones would radiate the divine life force into the new, transforming the ordinary into the extraordinary.

The Cathedral's foundation stone also carried national significance. The stone's composite structure symbolized promise. The spiritual power of an ancient faith was grafted into a youthful, energetic society, creating a unified force that would yield new service and accomplishment in the world. The foundation stone linked the Cathedral to the birthplace of Christianity. It demonstrated continuity over distance and time.

Perhaps the stone evidenced the spirit of Manifest Destiny, the 19th-century notion that the United States was divinely empowered to spread democracy throughout North America and beyond. The stone was set using "the mallet which President George Washington used at the laying of the cornerstone of the Capitol of the United States," while simultaneously, "a great American eagle hovered high in the sky directly above the foundation stone," recorded W. L. De Vries in *The Foundation Stone Book*.

W hy was it necessary to build the foundation of the Cathedral's altars first, rather than the exterior walls? The altar has primary importance because of its sacramental nature and ritualistic significance. As Cyril E. Pocknee explained in *The Christian Altar in History and Today*, "the temple exists for the altar and not the altar for the temple." Bishop Henry Yates Satterlee, the first bishop of the Episcopal Diocese of Washington, wrote in his *History of the Cathedral*, "the first stone of the Cathedral will be its stone altar." The altar is the *axis mundi*, the place that connects heaven and earth, where communion with God occurs, the center point around which revolve all actions, both sacred and profane. The altar should thus be the first element constructed in a new place of worship, and then the rest of the building put up around it.

Another question is why the foundation stone does not contain a time capsule, as was customary. De Vries expressed the view that a time capsule would indicate ". . . a lack of faith in the permanency of the building. As long as Mount St. Alban stands, Washington Cathedral is expected to stand." The builders did not intend for this stone ever to be removed.

Then, why was the foundation stone not placed where future generations could see and ponder it? De Vries wrote,

> . . . this is symbolic of the first beginning of the Incarnation, which the Church commemorates on the Feast of the Annunciation, and also of the Resurrection of our blessed Lord, two divine mysteries which were hidden from the human eye, as is God's way in his fresh beginnings of life, as well in the realms of nature as in the kingdom of grace.

Just as the foundation of the Christian tradition is based on unseen, divine mysteries, so is the foundation of this Cathedral based on the unseen support of its first stone.

Today we may also wonder what the first builders of the Cathedral hoped to achieve with this effort. Consider the ethos of the Episcopal Church at the time when the Cathedral was conceived. During the late 19th and early 20th centuries, the church was still influenced by the Oxford Movement and the Ecclesiological Society at Cambridge.

These efforts within the English church looked back to the Roman Catholic roots of Anglicanism, seeking to escape the corruption and ugliness of 19th-century church life by recapturing the piety, beauty, and splendor that were believed to have existed during the Middle Ages.

Theology influenced architecture, and the architectural style many believed appropriate for a new church building was Gothic Revival. In addition, highly liturgical forms of Christianity—Roman Catholic, Anglican, Lutheran, and Eastern Orthodox— considered sacred space less as a place where something is done, and more as a place where the divine is encountered.

Robert A. Scott explained in *The Gothic Enterprise* that medieval cathedrals (and by implication, "neo-Gothic" cathedrals) had two primary intentions. Cathedrals were

> . . . intended to mirror heaven as medieval theologians imagined it to be.
> . . . a setting in which humans could glimpse heaven, and thereby experience a foretaste of the hereafter.

Scott also expressed the view that

> . . . a cathedral is a place designed to draw the divine down among people; . . . by creating a congenial habitat for the divine; . . . akin to a great lens created to gather the diffuse ambient light of the divine spirit and focus it to a particular geographic location, where it becomes available for human worship and supplication.

The latter intention inspired the first builders of Washington National Cathedral as they fashioned the foundation stone and layered it with such levels of significance.

The creation and laying of the foundation stone was not, however, a singular, isolated incident in the Cathedral's construction. Its placement marked the beginning of a spiritual practice that extended over the following 83 years, until the last finial was placed. Stones from sacred places throughout the world—including the Western Wall on the Temple Mount, Canterbury, and Glastonbury—were incorporated into the building fabric. And visitors never tire of gazing at the sliver of rock from the moon in the Science and Technology Window (fondly called the Space Window), which invokes the whole mystery of God's universe. Many places thereby contributed to the spiritual construction of the building.

The Cathedral has not only incorporated sanctity from other places, but has already sent out sanctity of its own. In 1952, for example, a small

*"Father, in every age you have spoken through
the voices of prophets, pastors, and teachers.
Purify the lives and lips of those who speak here,
that your word only may be proclaimed,
and your word only may be heard."*

—*The Book of Common Prayer*

Reform Jewish congregation began meeting in the Cathedral's Bethlehem Chapel. By 1957, Temple Sinai had grown and was able to construct its own place of worship. The fabric of the synagogue includes not only a stone from a wall of the Temple of Herod Agrippa in Jerusalem, but also a stone from the building fabric of Washington National Cathedral, an instrumental place in this local Jewish congregation's spiritual growth and development. At the dedication ceremony, the congregation rose and said in unison,

> And this stone, which I have set up for a pillar, shall be God's house. May the significance of this ancient stone—drawn from the past and now being set in the present—serve through its strength as an inspiration for the welfare of our common future.

Faithful actions and sacred objects can help to make the Cathedral ever more a holy place as centuries pass. In the joining of a stone from Bethlehem with a block of American granite, ancient faith was grafted onto a house of worship built by a newer society. The invisible stone carries—upholds—the deepest yearning for relationship with God.

—*John Ander Runkle*

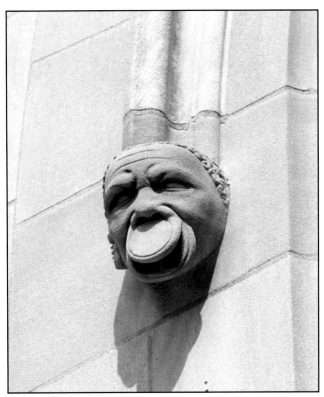

"Praise him with trumpet sound;
    praise him with the lute and harp!
Praise him with tambourine and dance;
    praise him with strings and pipe.
Praise him with clanging cymbals;
    praise him with loud clashing cymbals!"

—Psalm 150:3–5

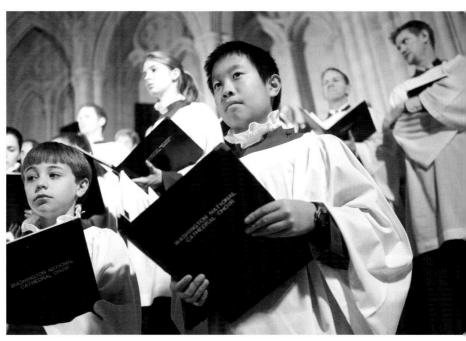

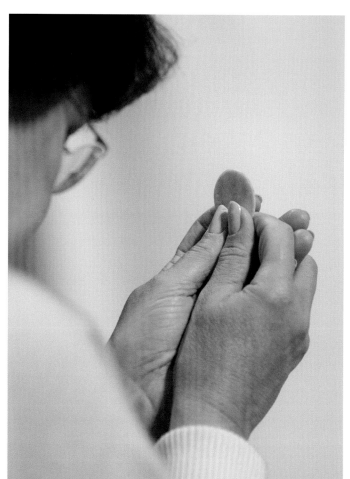

PIONEER FAITH

In September 1981, the month I took my oath of office as a United States Supreme Court Justice, I first saw Washington National Cathedral. The size and beauty of the place astonished me. It was as wonderful as any of the churches and cathedrals that I had seen in Europe, where my husband and I lived from 1954 to 1957.

Throughout adulthood, whenever I have moved, I have sought a church home. It was natural for me to inquire about Episcopal churches when we arrived in Washington. People told me that everyone, whether Episcopalian or not, should visit the Cathedral. That first visit led to a second, a few weeks later, when my husband and I attended worship. The service was familiar, although more formal than in the Southwest, where I grew up.

I was raised on the Lazy B, a remote cattle ranch that straddled southeastern Arizona and southwestern New Mexico. The ranch was far from any church. My father used to say that our church was the world around us. I shared his reverence for God's creation, and I prayed that God would send rain to help our cattle survive the dry desert existence.

Frontier life began to shape my family's beliefs long ago. My great-grandfather, John Price Hilton, founded a mission church in Wichita. He and his wife, Frances Sybil Hurnall Hilton, emigrated from England to Kansas. Both were Episcopalians steeped in high-church ways. Photographs show that they brought formal Victorian dress to the prairie.

Around January 1870, Rev. Hilton began to hold prayer services in Wichita, at the log home of Darius Munger. Although the Kansas frontier was thinly populated, Rev. Hilton quickly found settlers willing to donate land, materials, and labor to erect the first church of any kind in Wichita. Easter services were held there within just a few months.

The outside of that little mission church could hardly have been more different from the grandeur of Washington National Cathedral. The Protestant Episcopal Church of Wichita, which was later to be renamed

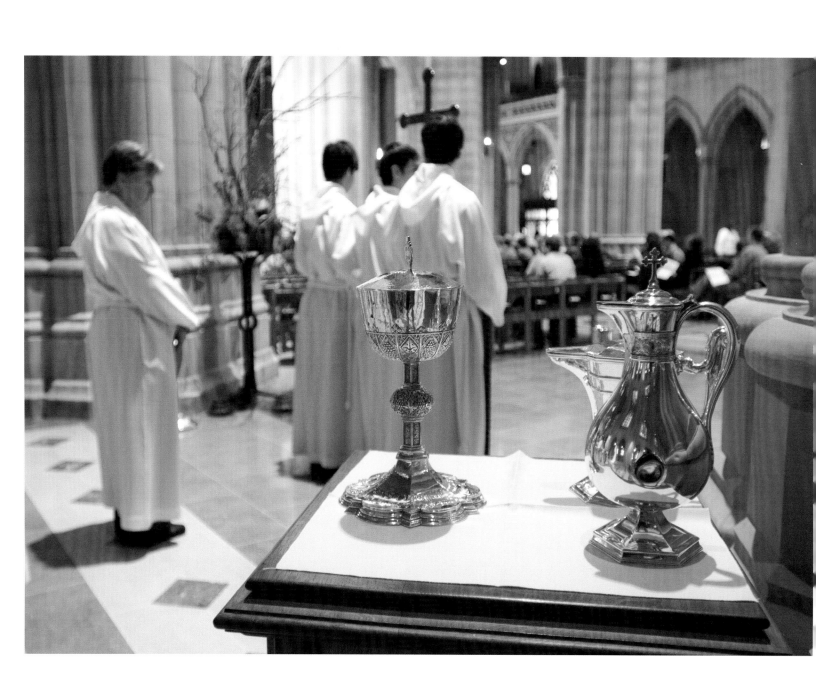

"For your presence whenever two or three have gathered together in your Name, we thank you, Lord."

—The Book of Common Prayer

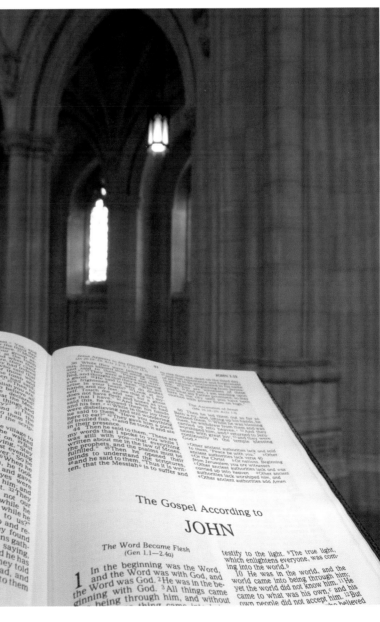

St. John's, measured only 16 feet by 35 feet. This adobe structure had a façade of cottonwood logs arranged in stockade fashion. In summertime, the dirt rooftop bloomed with a bountiful crop of sunflowers and prairie grass that waved in the breeze. Sybil Hilton worked tirelessly to make the church interior appealing. A rug covered the dirt floor, and worshipers sat on comfortable benches. Somehow an organ was procured.

Wichita grew rapidly in 1870. At the Hiltons' encouragement, other English immigrants settled in the region. St. John's invited people of all traditions, and locals and travelers alike flocked to the curious little house of worship. High-church Anglicans prayed alongside cowboys, gamblers, saloon keepers, a baker, musicians, attorneys, and the owner of a dry goods store. By all accounts, the vestry was a colorful lot.

As Christmas approached, St. John's was still the only completed church in town. It opened its doors wide for people of all ages and de-nominations to celebrate the birth of Jesus. The parish ladies decorated a Christmas tree with tinsel, candy, and small gifts for the children. Af-ter worship, the crowd walked to a nearby storehouse to feast on prairie chicken, venison, and other frontier treats.

The adobe church was always vulnerable to the harsh prairie climate, and after awhile it had to be abandoned. St. John's, now in a handsome stone building, continues to serve the people of Wichita.

The Hiltons' daughter Alice married my grandfather, Henry Clay "H. C." Day, a businessman from Vermont. In 1880 they moved to the southwest and founded the Lazy B. The ranch grew to more than 160,000 acres. H. C. owned some of the land and leased the rest from the federal government and the states of Arizona and New Mexico. Keeping the Lazy B required great ingenuity and toil, for resources were always scarce.

My father received some of his education in a one-room schoolhouse on the Lazy B. Public schools were later established, but at a considerable distance from our home. When I was six, my parents sent me to be educated in El Paso, Texas. I spent most academic years there, in the home of my maternal grandparents.

In El Paso I began to attend church regularly with my mother's sister, who took me to an Episcopal church, St. Clement's. I was confirmed in this tradition. By coincidence, that church was founded as a mission in 1870, the same year that St. John's was built in Wichita.

Shortly after I finished law school, my husband and I were married at the Lazy B by a priest from St. Clement's. We continued to worship regularly wherever we lived, and thus we found Washington National Cathedral in 1981. We met and admired the bishop, John Walker. Soon after his untimely death in 1989, I was invited to become a member of the Cathedral Chapter, now called the Board of Trustees. I had been determined not to undertake activities outside the Supreme Court because my work there was very demanding. Nevertheless, I agreed to join the Chapter.

I served on the Chapter for eight years, meeting all the people closely connected to the Cathedral and helping to address the needs of all the entities of the Close. Afterward I served on long-range planning committees, which framed the Cathedral's mission as a national house of prayer for all people. I agree with that concept. People from all across our country flock to Washington, D.C. Many of them visit the Cathedral as a part of their trip to our nation's capital city.

The Cathedral has always carried the Christian faith to frontiers of various kinds. A hundred years ago, Mount St. Alban was wooded and far from the bustle of downtown Washington; visitors can still experience some of that remoteness by walking through Olmsted Woods. Perhaps a more important kind of frontier is the Cathedral's ministry, which always explores the new and pressing challenges that our country faces.

For many years, the Cathedral has sought to include people of various religions in significant programs and services. In today's difficult times worldwide, these efforts are particularly important, because of the Cathedral's place in our capital, its history of receiving a Congressional charter, and its role as the place of worship during events of national concern.

Services are held at the Cathedral when a new president takes office, at times of tragedy and celebration, and to honor the lives of departed national leaders. At the funeral for President Reagan, I read a passage from John Winthrop's sermon preached in 1630, about his vision for religious freedom in America. Here too is evidence of pioneer faith:

> Now the only way . . . to provide for our posterity, is to follow
> the counsel of Micah, to do justly, to love mercy, to walk

humbly with our God.
. . . We must delight in
each other; make oth-
ers' conditions our own;
rejoice together, mourn
together, labor and
suffer together, always
having before our eyes
our commission and
community in the work,
as members of the same
body. . . . The Lord will
be our God, and delight
to dwell among us, as

His own people. . . . For we must consider that we shall be as a
city upon a hill. The eyes of all people are upon us. So that if
we shall deal falsely with our God in this work we have under-
taken, and so cause Him to withdraw His present help from us,
we shall be made a story and a by-word through the world.

The Cathedral follows Micah's counsel, and also supports private
searches for the divine. In my early years on the Supreme Court, I faced
many very challenging legal issues for which no perfect answer was
apparent. I sought God's guidance and blessing on many occasions during
all my years in Washington, D.C. Each time that I sought such guidance, I
felt strengthened and blessed by our Father's hand and spirit. I am
confident that my prayers were, and still are, heard.

In the 21st century, America will need spiritual aid to enable us to
avoid war and help the poor and dispossessed around the world. We must
use our strength and resources to strive for peace everywhere and reduce
suffering. I often think of the counsel found in Ecclesiastes (12:13): "Fear
God, and keep his commandments; for that is the whole duty of
everyone."

As our nation approaches new frontiers in an ever-changing world, the
Cathedral will be there for us, a symbol of eternity and steadfast beacon.
Visitors will find strength and sustenance in its beauty, its windows, its
carvings, its space, its music, its liturgy. Washington National Cathedral
continues to inspire me and to lead me to the light.

—Sandra Day O'Connor

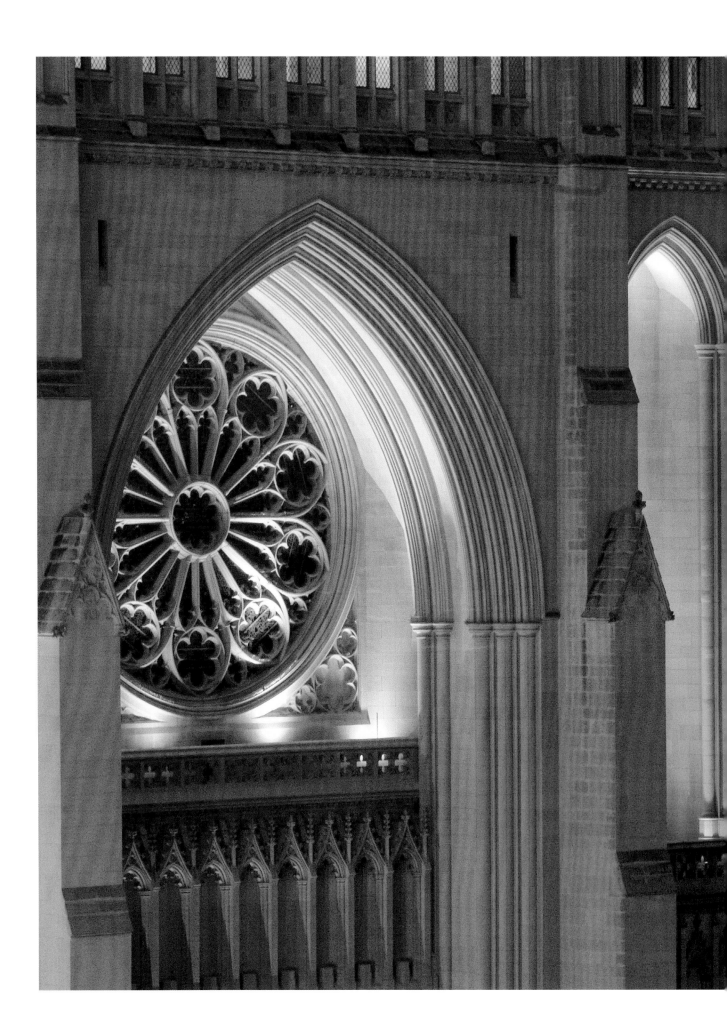

Look Up, and There It Is

I pass Washington National Cathedral every morning on my way to work, and again on the way home. I get to look at it from every angle and in every kind of weather. As I swim through the swirl of the "smartest people in the room" who make up Washington politics and the news business, the Cathedral acts as magnetic north for me. In fact, all who see the central tower can use it as a physical reminder to check their moral compasses.

It can't have been a mistake, or a surprise, for the people who planned and built the Cathedral as "a church for national purposes," that it might take the first step toward fulfilling a national purpose by just being there. The Cathedral's central tower is not the tallest structure in the District of Columbia, but because it stands on Mount St. Alban, it can be seen in ways the U.S. Capitol and the Washington Monument can't. That's a reminder: As important as we think we are, with our clout and knowledge, power and influence, there is always something more important.

I make my living as a reporter. I have spent my adult life going places not my own, and talking to people who are not my people. I gather quotes, stories, facts, and pictures from them. Then I turn around to face, through the camera's lens, yet another group of people, a mass group of strangers, and try to explain. I tell them what was happening to those other people, in that other place, what events meant to them, and what those strangers think of their situation.

Then I go home, sleep some, and do it all again the next day. That Cathedral tower in the distance, red warning lights blinking in concession to the needs of the modern age, is a place where a reporter's mission would be very well understood. Throw open the grand bronze gates. Gather in everyone who will come. Bring the tumult of the world. Embrace and challenge people of good will. Tell stories.

The preachers, teachers, seekers, artists, healers, and repairers who bring their work to those gathered inside can never know for sure what impact they have had. Afterward, the great doors close, and the lights are dimmed. And the next morning, the Cathedral awakens to do it all over again.

I can see the Cathedral for miles on my way home, drenched in sunlight or swathed in mist. Its serene bulk is reassuring, while inside after

countless visits I am as dazzled as a tourist who has walked the short distance from the bus for a first look at the place.

Because I am an Episcopalian, I might be a little more at home than many casual first-time visitors. I've headed inside the Cathedral to welcome the new year with lessons and carols, to hear great preaching and beautiful music on the festival days of our faith, and to watch as friends are commissioned and anointed to perform important ministries of the church. So I know something about the work of the place, its ministries and hopes.

The Cathedral has worked very hard over the years to be more than a place shown on the news at Christmas and Easter, and the nation's altar in times of crisis and mourning. At these tasks this "house of prayer for all people" succeeds magnificently, but it is so much more than that.

During an interview that I once conducted, the Rev. Altagracia Perez, an Episcopal priest from Los Angeles County, said something in passing that has stuck with me ever since: "The church needs to be a place where people come together and have conversations that are hard."

The idea has stuck with me because it is simple, and right. And it has stuck with me as I have worked with the Cathedral, because this century-old place of beauty and worship also wants to pull you in off the streets of Washington D.C., the United States, and the world to have hard conversations.

I need the church in my life to find a place of quiet just inside the doors from the howling winds of the world. A lifetime in the church has made an adult lifetime in the news business possible, offering another way,

besides the "world's way," to make sense of it all.

Think of it as two-way traffic: I bring the world trailing behind me, clanking like a string of tin cans tied to my ankle even as I quietly try to make my way down that long nave to a good seat near the altar. The church offers a way to look at the world out there and one's place in it.

At the same time I bring the church back out to the world with me, inside me, where my dealings with both the great names and the powerless among us are tempered by what the church has taught me all my life.

Faith informs vocation in my dealings with the world. As a reporter, I am constantly meeting a wide slice of the human family, asking them questions, and having the answers inform the way I tell their story to others.

Who are these people to me? Presidents, welfare recipients, prime ministers, gang boys, cardinals, intravenous drug users, ward bosses, construction workers, academics? Am I using them as props? When I turn the camera on them, do I give the impoverished the same privilege of self-protection that I might be expected to give the powerful or wealthy? Do their personal stories belong to me? Are they mine to do with what I choose? These are some of the knottiest problems I face. From the answers to these questions I can build what might be called an ethic of self-presentation, granting the privilege of equal dignity to the people I interview.

The way my faith asks me to be—*in the world* but not *of the world*—can't help but guide my professional behavior. My faith forces me constantly to consider the treatment and the personal sovereignty of the people I meet in my work. It would be easier to write people off and take from them what I need and move on. It might be a better career move to curry favor with people at the other end of the continuum, give them better treatment because they are somehow "better"—but I can't do that.

I save special respect and empathy for those people who aren't welcoming my camera into their lives just because they want something from me. I have to protect them, to treat them differently from the people who enter into a transaction with me at the newsroom because they are trying to get something: a leg up on their rivals, a shot at my audience, more publicity for their book.

Religious life gives me a sure anchor during crises in my business, and crises in the lives of the communities I've covered. I've seen people at their best, most noble and decent, and I've seen them at their worst. I've seen the bad things, the famines, the murder victims, the fraud trials, the looting after riots, the flood- and tornado-ravaged towns. I've seen the sufferings of the people I've covered, and I come away from those encounters amazed at the great and sustaining faith people have. If put to the test in the same way, would my faith be as strong?

I thought the news business would put money in my pocket, get me far beyond Brooklyn, give me a chance to see the world, and talk to the people who make that daily life tick. I've been transported by the roar of a hundred thousand people in a soccer stadium as Nelson Mandela raised his fist at the final rally before South Africa's first free elections. I've experienced the nasty tension of being on the wrong end of a police raid in Uzbekistan as I tried to interview members of the political opposition. I once bumped into the Pope as—against the advice of his doctors—he checked himself out of the hospital after the attempt on his life. I've been thrown to the ground by the force of a blast when a parked Mercedes was blown to bits as I stood with a crowd in Lesotho. I've covered elections in Mexico and the aftermath of Hurricane Katrina.

"The church needs to be a place where people come together and have conversations that are hard."

My career has allowed me to be immersed up to my eyeteeth in the joys and sorrows of the world, and to live a life that makes me a perpetual student. Unlike many people, I do my daily work in front of millions of witnesses. I do my work having made an implied contract with the people who are watching and listening, that I will try to give them a picture of the state of the world that is not prearranged, that will not be designed to push the viewer toward one conclusion or another.

I come to this work with a sense of duty or vocation that I believe is very similar to the vocation of those who choose the religious life. Ours are both "not just jobs." They are whole ways of seeing the world. They are both jobs bound by abstracts in which the priest and the journalist say, "Give me something really valuable: your trust."

As a reporter, I can't explain everything. At some point I have to hope I have a deposit of trust to draw on. I can't demand it. I can only ask for it, and hope that I've banked enough with my readers and viewers to give me credence.

I have spent my life groping forward, trying to discern what God wants from me and from his creation. The gift of a mind that's not all made up has helped me in this, and made me a better reporter at the same time. I can echo with confidence the young Mary who exclaims in Luke's Gospel, that "he who is mighty has done great things for me" (1:49*a*). I strive to live out the very clear assignment Jesus gave in Matthew (25:34*b*–36):

> Come, you that are blessed by my Father, inherit the kingdom prepared for you from the foundation of the world; for I was hungry and you gave me food, I was thirsty and you gave me something to drink, I was a stranger and you welcomed me, I was naked and you gave me clothing, I was sick and you took care of me, I was in prison and you visited me.

We do not want our reporters to be evangelists, so I have to concentrate more on doing these things than talking about them. Here in Washington, where saying something is routinely mistaken for doing it, that's probably a good thing.

My Cathedral, our Cathedral, beckons us both inside its doors. We will meet there, you and I, in all our human frailty and imperfect vision, in all our hearts' longings for ourselves and for the world. It is a relief to have a place to lay aside the grasping and hustling. It is a relief to leave a world where conflict is a kind of currency to leverage and spend. It is a relief to walk through the Cathedral's great doors where conflict is not wished away but instead is understood to be a state far short of the happiness that the One who made us longs to be ours.

—*Ray Suarez*

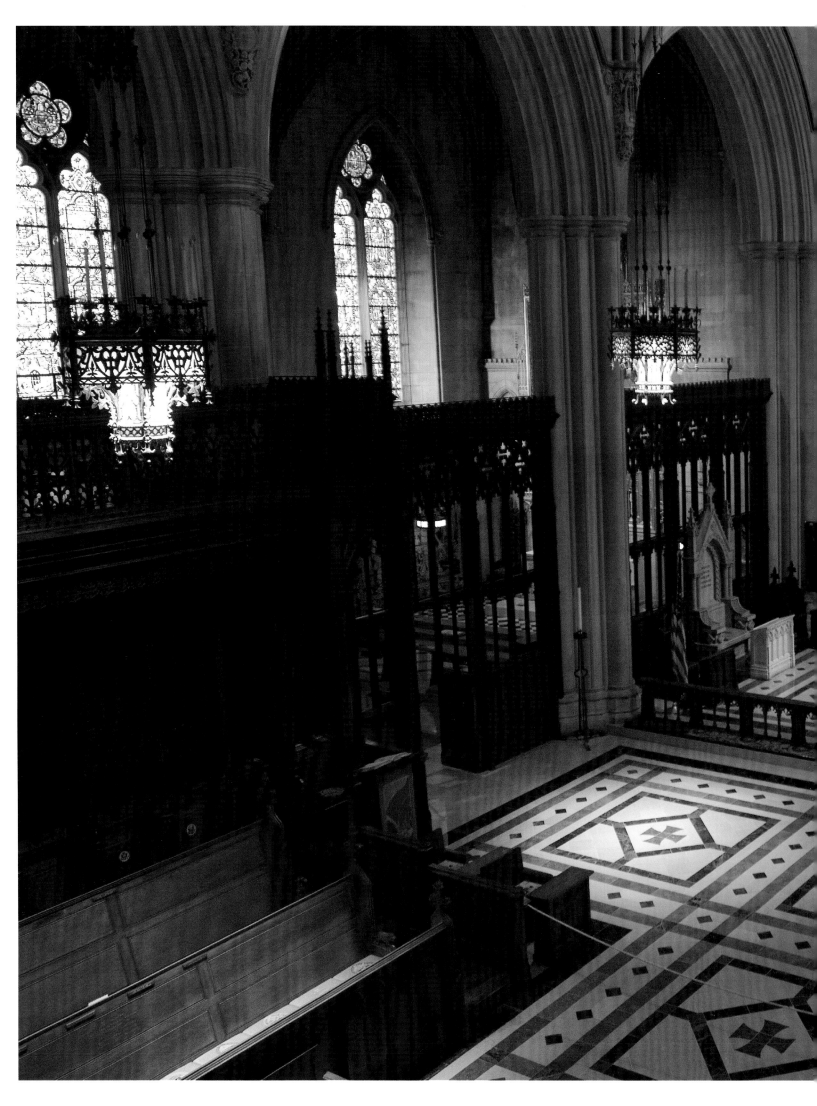

Essayists

Samuel T. Lloyd III was installed as the ninth dean of Washington National Cathedral in 2005. He previously served as rector of historic Trinity Church, Copley Square, in Boston, Massachusetts.

Diane Ney, an accomplished author and playwright, serves as an archivist and historian at Washington National Cathedral.

Sandra Day O'Connor served as associate justice of the United States Supreme Court from 1981 to 2006. She has volunteered as a member of the governing board of the Cathedral Foundation.

John Ander Runkle is the conservator at Washington National Cathedral. He is both an Episcopal priest and an architect.

Ray Suarez, senior correspondent for *The NewsHour with Jim Lehrer* on PBS, is a past member of the National Advisory Committee of Washington National Cathedral.

Editors

Margaret Bergan Davis, project director

Gregory A. Rixon, managing editor

Donovan Marks, art director

Amy C. Babcock, editor

List of Illustrations

All photos by Donovan Marks except as stated below.

Designer
Donovan Marks

Technical Designer
Craig W. Stapert

Typeface
Goudy Old Style

Printed by
Peake DeLancey Printers, LLC
Cheverly, Maryland

The editors are indebted to
Diane Ney
Margaret Shannon
C. Evan Davies, archivist of the Episcopal Diocese of the Rio Grande
Kathleen Pott, historian of St. John's Episcopal Church of Wichita